Good Gauley!

Whitewater Rafting in West Virginia

Katie Sharp

Rigby

A Harcourt Achieve Imprint

www.Rigby.com
1-800-531-5015

Some sports can be done only in certain places. Imagine surfing without waves, mountain climbing without mountains, or downhill skiing without snowy hills. Certain sports require certain types of **geography**.

Different landforms allow people to do many exciting sports.

One sport that depends on geography is **whitewater** rafting. This thrilling sport takes place on the ever-moving water of a river.

Curtis has never been whitewater rafting, but he would like to go someday. He and his mother often go online to learn more about whitewater rafting. Curtis also writes emails to a river guide.

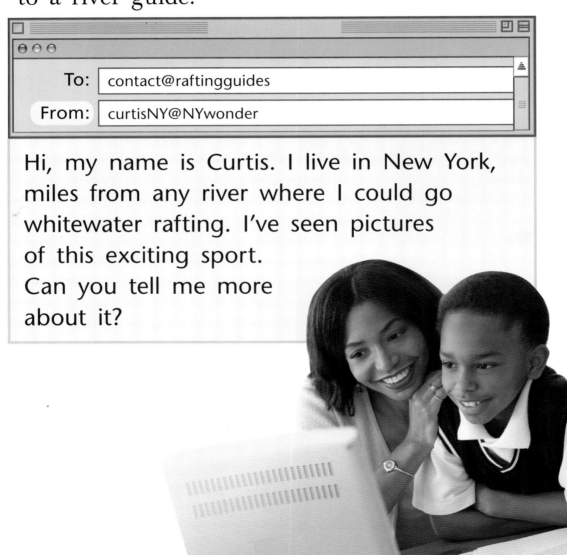

To: contact@raftingguides

From: curtisNY@NYwonder

Hi, my name is Curtis. I live in New York, miles from any river where I could go whitewater rafting. I've seen pictures of this exciting sport. Can you tell me more about it?

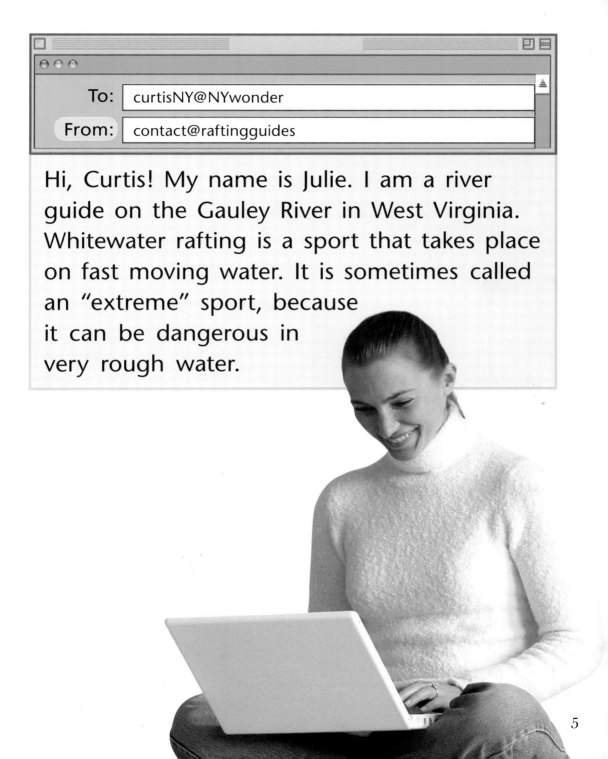

To: curtisNY@NYwonder

From: contact@raftingguides

Hi, Curtis! My name is Julie. I am a river guide on the Gauley River in West Virginia. Whitewater rafting is a sport that takes place on fast moving water. It is sometimes called an "extreme" sport, because it can be dangerous in very rough water.

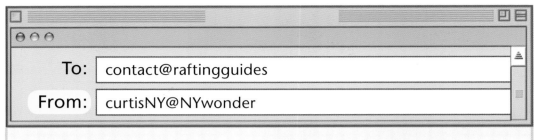

To: contact@raftingguides

From: curtisNY@NYwonder

Hi, Julie. I've never heard of the Gauley River. Can you tell me more about it?

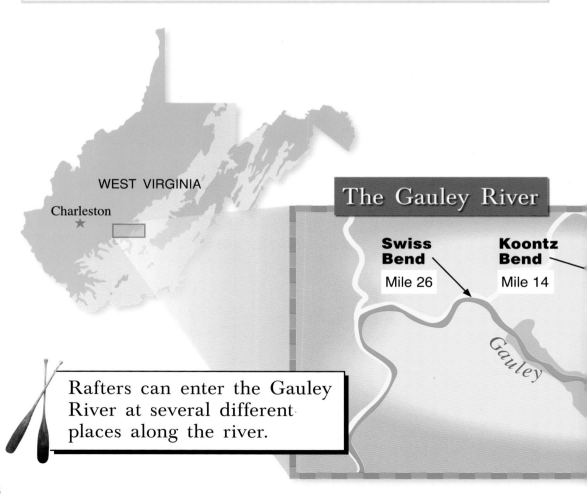

WEST VIRGINIA

Charleston

The Gauley River

Swiss Bend

Mile 26

Koontz Bend

Mile 14

Gauley

Rafters can enter the Gauley River at several different places along the river.

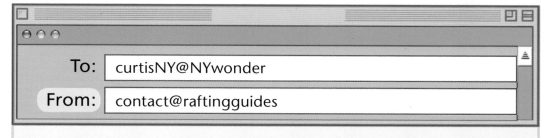

The Gauley River begins as a creek in the Appalachian Mountains. It flows south and west, stretching down through steep and rocky **canyon** walls. At the town of Gauley Bridge, it joins with the New River. The rivers combine to form the Kanawha River.

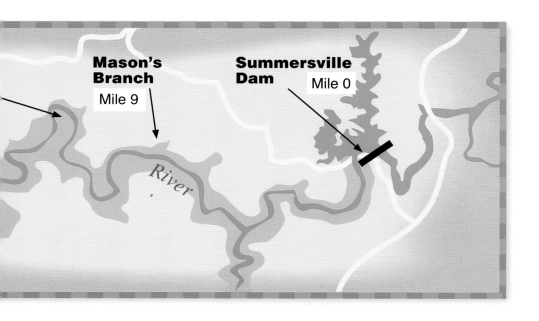

Mason's Branch
Mile 9

Summersville Dam
Mile 0

River

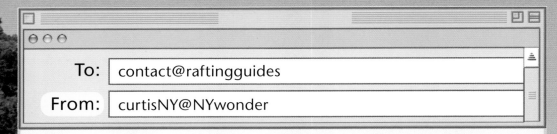

To: contact@raftingguides

From: curtisNY@NYwonder

The Gauley River sounds really cool. I love being around water! Can beginners like me enjoy whitewater rafting? What kinds of special equipment do you need?

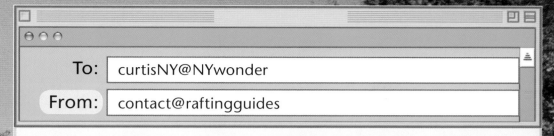

Beginners can enjoy whitewater rafting on some of the easier rivers. The youngest rafters are usually around 11 years old, while many people wait to begin rafting until they are at least 16 years old.

Paddlers need a small boat, paddles, a life jacket and helmet, and a first aid kit. And beginners definitely need a guide!

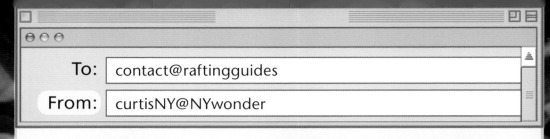

To: contact@raftingguides

From: curtisNY@NYwonder

Why is it so important to have a river guide with you? Can you explain what river guides do?

River guides help keep whitewater rafters safe.

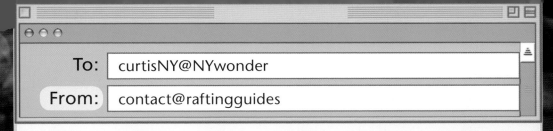

To: curtisNY@NYwonder

From: contact@raftingguides

River guides teach paddlers how to sit in the raft, use a paddle, and steer through waves and rocks in the **rapids**. Another very important part of their job is keeping everyone safe. They also enjoy sharing fun facts about the people, places, and critters that call the river home.

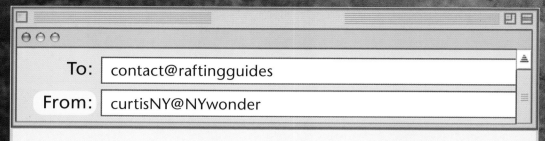

To: contact@raftingguides

From: curtisNY@NYwonder

I told my dad and mom about the Gauley River. They want to know more about it. Can you tell me about the geography around there?

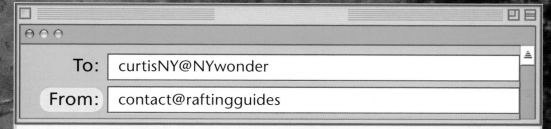

To: curtisNY@NYwonder

From: contact@raftingguides

Because the Gauley River is in the mountains, it has many steep slopes. Over time, the river water has cut through the hard rock to form **gorges**, canyons, and ridges. The river itself is often filled with large rocks. The rocks can make it difficult to steer a raft because you have to go around them. But they also make whitewater rafting more fun!

Rafters enjoy beautiful scenery as they travel down the Gauley River.

To: contact@raftingguides

From: curtisNY@NYwonder

I looked at pictures of the Gauley River on the Internet. It looks awesome. I guess that's why people love rafting on the Gauley.

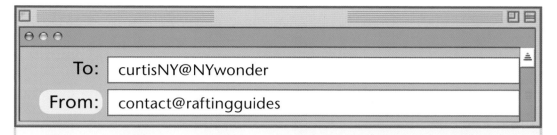

To: curtisNY@NYwonder

From: contact@raftingguides

There are many reasons to love the Gauley River. It's clean, cold, narrow, steep, and winding. Few rivers have all that. And the twenty-mile stretch that paddlers travel offers nonstop action with some of the biggest waves, steepest drops, and most difficult rapids of any river. The Gauley River is unmatched anywhere in the United States.

People choose to raft on the Gauley because of its fast and exciting rapids.

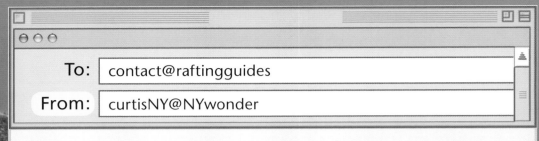

To: contact@raftingguides

From: curtisNY@NYwonder

My dad, mom, and I are really interested in rafting on the Gauley River in a few years when I am older. What time of year is best to go rafting?

You may want to come in the fall to see when water is released from the nearby Summersville **Dam**. This sends a rush of more than 20,000 gallons of water every second into the river. That water creates rapids unlike any found on other rivers.

Water released from a dam upstream creates rapids that are great for rafting.

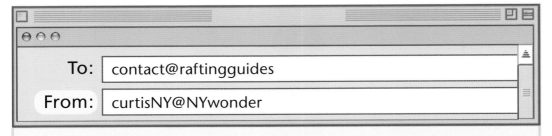

To: contact@raftingguides

From: curtisNY@NYwonder

Wow! That sounds incredible. Why is all that water released from the dam each fall? It's not just to make whitewater rafting more fun, is it?

When the dam was built, it created a lake. Each fall water is released to make space in the lake for rainfall and to prevent flooding. At first the release happened too quickly. There was too much water for safe paddling. Now it's released over six weekends to give paddlers more chances to enjoy the sport.

This lake was created by a dam built on the Gauley River.

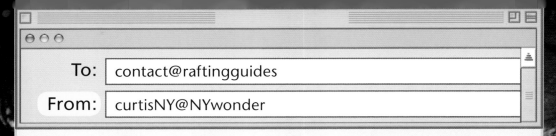

To: contact@raftingguides

From: curtisNY@NYwonder

Whitewater rafting sounds like a lot of fun, but it sounds kind of dangerous, too. Is it?

Lots can happen when paddlers bounce downstream in a raft. A wave can hit the boat, bumping a paddler out. Or the boat can flip—and then everyone's in the water. That's why it's important to wear a life jacket and helmet and listen to instructions from your guide!

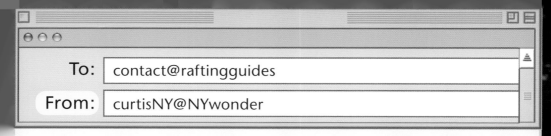

To: contact@raftingguides

From: curtisNY@NYwonder

I'm so excited! My parents have agreed to plan a trip. We're going whitewater rafting! Thanks for all the helpful information, Julie. I learned a lot about whitewater rafting and the Gauley River! I can't wait to hit the rapids.

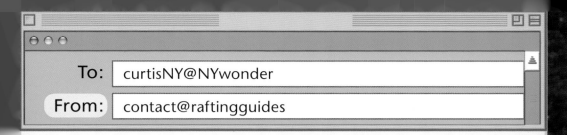

To: curtisNY@NYwonder

From: contact@raftingguides

You're welcome, Curtis! It sounds like you and your family have something to look forward to. If you visit the Gauley River make sure to stop by and say hi!

Glossary

canyon a deep valley with high, steep sides

dam something put across a river or stream to limit or prevent the water's flow

geography the study of the earth's surface and the living things on it

gorges deep, narrow canyons or valleys

rapids an area on a river where the water moves very quickly

whitewater bubbly, white water that is found on rapids